ABOUT DECORATING

THE REMARKABLE ROOMS OF
RICHARD KEITH LANGHAM

ABOUT DECORATING

THE REMARKABLE ROOMS OF
RICHARD KEITH LANGHAM

BY SARA RUFFIN COSTELLO

PRINCIPAL PHOTOGRAPHY BY TREL BROCK

RIZZOLI
NEW YORK

New York · Paris · London · Milan

Contents

OTHER PEOPLE'S ROOMS

I am perhaps the least materialistic person I know. I do not own one proper or pedigreed object, painting, or piece of furniture—I suppose that's because I could never begin to afford the rarified things that I (a veritable "village peddler," which is one of my nicknames) sell to my clients. My apartment in the city and my ramshackle house in Water Mill on Long Island are full of sentimental and quirky junk—so you will most definitely *not* be seeing any of my rooms in these pages.

What you will see is a varied array of other people's rooms that I've had the adventure and privilege to help create over my career. For over thirty years I have scavenged the world over to find beautiful things, and assembled them in beautiful rooms in beautiful houses in beautiful places. My method has really never deviated over these many years. I have never followed a trend nor paid the slightest attention to the newest thing. I conceive these rooms from my instinct coupled with some "innate vision" I was blessed (or cursed) to be born with. Having learned the art of decoration from two masters (Mark Hampton and Keith Irvine) early on, I still do it the old-fashioned way—dreaming up the room and adding each element piece by piece to achieve a finished result that has personality, suitability, and depth. I want my rooms to recognize the past, just in a somewhat fresher interpretation.

The process of decorating is exciting, stimulating, and hugely satisfying, but it can also be long, arduous, and a tad frustrating. I love all the ingredients in a room—the grain of good wood, the luster of gilding, the drape of fabric, the silhouette of furniture, and the play of color and pattern. I want my rooms to be exciting and comfortable, and to really suit the location and the people who inhabit them. The thrill for me is to see all the elements finally come together. When years of paint samples and sawdust and site meetings come to an end, it is satisfying to see what started as just a house turn into that most precious of all places—home.

—Richard Keith Langham
New York, New York

TIME REGAINED

This long-time family home in Hattiesburg, Mississippi, is a Proustian temple of memories for its homeowners and their decorator. Three decades ago, a pair of young newlyweds acquired a Low Country–style starter house. Lewis Graeber III, their architect from the Mississippi Delta, urged the couple to fly up to New York and interview Irvine & Fleming (Langham's employer at the time) to decorate. At the same time, Langham was also whispering in his boss's ear, "If they like us, I want to oversee the job!" As it turned out, the couple hired Irvine & Fleming, Langham decorated the house, and the homeowners were thrilled.

Cut to ten years later. The couple's children were growing fast, and again Langham was called down South—this time to decorate an addition. Another victory! Several more years pass with intermittent spruce-ups, when along came hurricane Katrina, ripping through his clients' beloved house and decimating the property's population of ancient pine trees. After the devastation was cleared, the family ultimately decided to rebuild, but were divided on how to proceed; the husband wished to construct a larger, more elegantly scaled house and the wife generally wished for everything to return to how it was. In the end, they both triumphed; Graeber rebuilt on roughly the same footprint, introducing taller ceilings, a grander entrance hall, and a light-filled gallery/hallway that connects the house end to end. And Langham, who at this point was almost as emotionally connected to these rooms as his clients were, knew intuitively that the original spirit of the house must be restored.

They began with the jewel in the crown: the cypress-paneled living room. Langham remembers, "The deeper we got into redesigning that room with its exquisite pickled paneling, mellow and chalky with gilt highlighting, we remembered how lovely it felt to actually be in there and we just wanted to go back." The desire to improve but not change (too much) ultimately drove most of the design solutions. "We really just wound up following the threads of our collective memories; the light, the colors, and the moods associated with our time spent in both the grand spaces and the private, cozy corners of this wonderful new, old house."

The view from the pickled cypress-paneled living room toward the front door. "We wanted a non-color in the entrance vestibule so that the other three rooms off it could announce themselves properly." Surrounding the walnut center table are four elaborately painted klismos-style chairs from England. Creamy woodwork and Cotswold limestone temper the richness of mocha walls.

ABOVE: Portieres line one side of the house's main artery, buffering the adjacent living room from the bright Mississippi sunshine streaming in through French doors. **OPPOSITE:** A Cole & Son damask paper wraps around the double-height stair hall while dozens of painted dogs (inspired by a similar gallery of pictures Albert Hadley installed at Brooke Astor's country house) look on. A local woodworker—who showed up every day with a parrot sitting on his shoulder—masterfully constructed the exquisite flying stairway, which Langham brought to life with a burnt-pomegranate runner. **FOLLOWING SPREAD:** The living room was resolutely returned to how it was. Cypress paneling from the original incarnation was pickled, once again by Bruce Nettles, a cocoa color and trimmed with thin lines of glimmering gold leaf. The contemporary Georgian sofa, covered in mallard-green velvet, wakes up a traditional floor plan by sitting with its back to the portieres that divide the drawing room from the gallery. "We wanted this room to feel aged, handsome, and mellow," Langham says. Ultimately, the entire palette for the house—ivory, mocha, tobacco, salmon, and jade—was found in the living room's made-to-order Bessarabian carpet.

ABOVE: With his clients' frequent parties in mind, Langham whittled out several seating areas in the living room. Here a sinuous Langham & Company armless slipper sofa and salon chair offer a secluded reprieve from the main cluster. Besides the carpet, the salon chair's leafy green and turquoise chintz is the only other bold pattern in the room, but even it is mellowed by a pale check on its outside back.
OPPOSITE: A collection of creamware fills the antique breakfront, and an oversize hexagonal table—a repository for piles of books and a lantern—is layered with a Kashmir paisley shawl thrown over a persimmon silk skirt.

ABOVE: Finding matching antiques to flank the dining room entrance proved to be a challenge. "We fell in love with this Adam mirror and period commode we found in England, but of course the dealer only had one of each," Langham remembers. "Luckily, he also had a workshop in Yorkshire who was able to make miraculous copies!" **RIGHT:** After remodeling, the height of the dining room ceiling jumped from nine to twelve feet, making the larger expanse of wall an ideal canvas for a panoramic Gracie mural of the meandering Mississippi River. Curtains, with festoons and jabots, are made of emerald-green silk and drip with tobacco fringe. The dining room table, which seats sixteen, was bought directly off the showroom floor of Thomas Goode & Co., London's foremost tableware emporium. Mismatched chairs add personality.

ABOVE: Lacquered walls are juxtaposed with the matte surface of the magnificent Adam mantelpiece found at Nigel Bartlett while shopping in England. Bookcase backs are lined in tactile Ultrasuede. OPPOSITE: A French Empire gilt-wood chandelier–whose chain is coiled with a cinnabar-colored wool cord and finished at the ceiling with a velvet collar and cap–hovers low over the library table. Four Georgian library chairs (two are original and two are copies) wear midnight-blue waxed leather with an opposing silk check on their outside backs. FOLLOWING SPREAD: A magnificent Sultanabad carpet, woven with a huge pattern, moderates the cacophony of tartans, florals, and kilims in the family room. "We found the rug and built the room from there." The six-foot-square coffee table with saber legs, made by a local craftsman in Hattiesburg, was designed after a narrow Regency hall bench.

A screened porch is practically a requirement in the South. The wicker chairs are from Leslie Curtis, who makes marvelous reproductions, and the chestnut-topped dining table was crafted in Memphis by Robert Johnson. Besides antiques, much of the furniture and lighting Langham uses is custom made; that way the dimensions, the shape, and the mood are controlled. The painted tole lantern is one of a kind, snagged on a shopping trip in Atlanta.

ABOVE: Constellations of blue-and-white Delft plates scattered across apple-green walls riff off the original breakfast room's color scheme. Vases on brackets hold seasonal flora. **OPPOSITE:** The nineteenth-century dhurrie rug was cut, and its border re-seamed, to perfectly fit the shape of the room. Chairs that previously lived in the old dining room were re-covered and given new life around the breakfast table. Langham designed the light fixture, complete with Delft candlesticks mounted on a wooden ring and topped with midnight-blue linen shades.

ABOVE: A strong romantic spirit imbues the master bedroom's sitting area, though it remains grounded due in part to walls hung with soothing, dark chocolate, paperbacked silk—even the pink lacquered ceiling doesn't seem to tip the scales. As determined and glamorous as the palette is, somehow a small mink-trimmed ottoman steals the show. **OPPOSITE:** Heavy silk curtains, sewn in New York and shipped down to Hattiesburg, are trimmed with chocolate piping and three layers of pinking-sheared ruffles in green, aquamarine, and rose. A not-too-sweet, vintage Colefax and Fowler chintz-covered armchair pulls up to the antique writing desk. **FOLLOWING SPREAD:** In a deliberate attempt to keep the master bedroom mostly unchanged from its original design, Langham had the same Cole & Son pale aqua wallpaper remade. The elongated California king-size bed ("a much prettier shape than a regular square king") is copied after a Chippendale design and hung with striped satin. Unlined curtains, also in pale aquamarine silk to seamlessly blend with the walls, have a delicate Penn & Fletcher embroidered border. For blackout, matelassé night curtains, installed underneath, electronically close across the windows.

ABOVE: In her master bath, iridescent ivory moiré wallpaper is surrounded by woodwork glazed a baby-aspirin color. The pretty French-blue valence speaks directly to a delicate little eighteenth-century chair. **OPPOSITE:** Peekaboo blush curtains made of linen and silk organza and bordered with tiny pearls are romantic, dramatic, and deeply feminine. Local artisan Kym Garraway-Braley designed and painted the soft geometric pattern on the floor.

TROPICAL PUNCH

O cean-front properties rarely come up for sale on Waspy Jupiter Island (or "Hobe Sound," as insiders insist) and are generally passed down from one generation to the next. So when an architecturally challenged 1970s contemporary one day appeared on the market—despite friends' cries of "Please no!"—Langham's client and his partner jumped on the opportunity. One of the pair, a native of Chattanooga, Tennessee, had grown up spending holidays at his family's vacation house on Vero Beach and was nostalgic to re-create a similar, old-fashioned experience.

Local architect George Bollis was brought in to steer the house toward a more old-world Florida vernacular while Langham set about designing a wintertime oasis, surrounded by citrus and palm trees, that would look as though it had been standing for a hundred years. To promote a happy, seaside feeling Langham held up two important criteria. First, the color palette ought to align with the traditional pinks, greens, and blues of Harbour Island and Bermuda: pale shell, shrimp, salmon, coral, citrus, melon, jade, palm, and the turquoise blues of the sea. And second, seating arrangements must be capacious enough for a large group but also intimate enough for two.

The designer mined his East Coast Country Club vocabulary, selecting plenty of wicker, rattan, and caned pieces as well as whiffs of Anglo-Indian and preppy exoticism. In one of the master suites and dressing rooms, Langham riffed off the newly installed Chinese Chippendale railings by incorporating a trove of chinoiserie shapes, fabric, and fretwork wallpaper.

Afternoon scavenger hunts in the antiques stores along South Dixie Highway produced a haul of regional one-of-a-kind treasures—always updated with fresh fabric or coat of lacquer—that corresponded to the "we've been here for ages" aesthetic. The homeowners' ceramic bird collection and paintings of landscapes and animals helped to further situate the rooms in the leafy Everglades. The project was finished in less than a year and the formerly charm-free house miraculously transformed into an elegant grande dame decorated, but not *too* decorated. Like a good facelift, the results are triumphant; no one can tell how much work went in, just that she looks very good for her age.

On the inland side of the house, a travertine path bordered by meticulous landscaping is punctuated by a pair of grand old Floridian lattice doors, perfectly articulating a patrician island tone.

ABOVE: Specimen prints of tropical fruits, a curious pair of painted tole palm-tree lamps, and the homeowners' ceramic bird collection hint at what's to come. **OPPOSITE:** Regulation thirty-two-inch-square games tables do not allow much extra elbow room, so Langham commissioned a forty-inch-square one instead—and had it wrapped in linen and glazed.

LEFT: Instead of a formal dining room off the kitchen, the home-owners asked for a secondary, more private living room. The L-shaped Turkish sofa delivers loungy comfort while scatter pillows in mint, cantaloupe, and grapefruit complement the tropical palette. Whitewashed pecky cypress walls and aquamarine fabric-backed linen crisply finish the tropical narrative. FOLLOWING SPREAD: In the main sitting room, blue-green walls reference the sea while an evocative Alice Ludwig landscape settles the room heroically. Block-printed slipcovers and mismatched rattan chairs feel nostalgic, relaxing the formality.

ABOVE: The living room is divided into three generous seating areas. A pair of caned sofas works the middle while a grouping of upholstered chairs and a round pedestal dining table (not pictured) anchor either side. Each arrangement sits atop its own candy-striped dhurrie whose stripes alternate by their placement—running vertically, then horizontally, and then vertically again. Handmade locally, the fretwork cabinet is painted salt-water salmon and crowned with a nautilus shell finial. **OPPOSITE:** Custom made in Louisiana from harvested "sinker" cypress wood (petrified logs submerged over hundreds of years on river bed bottoms) the six-foot-round colonial dining table elegantly weathers the scars of time. For that reason, a heavy marble urn filled with palm fronds poses no threat to the table's surface. A set of Bielecky Brothers rattan chairs (made in the Bronx since 1903) speaks the same genuine language, and sheer linen curtains appropriately situate the room seaside.

A coveted spot for ocean breezes, the balcony off the living room was designed to provide treetop views of sunrise and moonrise over the Atlantic. The wicker chairs, ottoman, and splat-arm banquette's upholstery all accentuate the country-club aesthetic.

"Everyone is happy in a Florida vacation house," Langham laughs. Uneven kitchen cabinets, monkey wallpaper, and a series of ceramic simian overlords promote good humor. The terra-cotta floor tiles are glazed white and jade, and the Urban Electric light fixtures are painted in cabana stripes. Shrimp pink on the ceiling visually connects with the deep coral in the adjacent sitting room.

OPPOSITE: In the entranceway to the master bedroom, driftwood boards painted with a swamp scene plus Philip Jeffries jungle-green grass-cloth wallpaper evoke old Florida. ABOVE: A ceramic giraffe perpetually kneels in the shade of a 1920s painted tole palm tree.

Saturated mango walls and
a lime-green bed are both
neutralized by a soothing cotton
twill carpet laid over bleached
wood floors. Quirky bedside
tables, plucked from a junk shop
on South Dixie Highway, are
coated in leaf-green lacquer.

Basic windows are elevated by
Langham's custom pagoda-
shaped pelmets and are dressed
with an archival Kent-Bragaline
print on linen. Bailey & Griffin
stripes cover the chair while the
entire seating area is enlivened
with tassel-trimmed side tables
in an unexpected peacock blue.

ABOVE: A cocoon of luxury is spun around an imperial four-poster bed, originally designed in the 1970s by Sister Parish. Gauzy ombréd curtains and a Fortuny box spring and canopy enclose the room-within-a-room. A flush of coral color peeks out from underneath while the television hides inside a custom console, also upholstered in coral, at the foot of the bed. The entire concoction fits neatly into a mirrored niche studded with gilt rosettes. OPPOSITE: A limed-oak English partners desk anchors the room handsomely and also serves as a kind of neutral bridge, connecting differently hued furniture. Above the desk, Alice Ludwig's giraffes silently forage.

ABOVE: JAB fabric transports the bunkroom into a snorkeling adventure through sea fans and coral. Even the trompe-l'oeil chest of drawers gets the deep-sea treatment. Additionally, vivid turquoise covers the floor and ceiling and is splashed up under the top bunk. **OPPOSITE:** Langham sourced glazed concrete tiles in Miami and asked the vendor to stencil a few with starfish. The ten-foot-tall bamboo and rattan bed was custom built by Bamboo & Rattan in West Palm Beach and the "Dilly Dally Down Dare" fish sign was snagged on Harbour Island and hung in the guest cabana as a reminder to relax. **FOLLOWING SPREAD:** Sea-horse sentries enforce a strict code of symmetry in the pool house and help to dial up the vintage Slim Aarons appeal.

UPSTAIRS DOWNSTAIRS

Longing for a relaxed pace, away from the hustle of New York City, where he had been burning the midnight oil at Goldman Sachs for twenty years, Langham's client was mulling over a decision to relocate to a farm in rural Virginia. When asked what he thought about this development, Langham politely remarked, "Have you lost your mind?" (The client was also a dear pal, whom Langham sensed would have a difficult time completely leaving the razzle-dazzle of city life behind.) After a few months spent in the remote countryside, the young man came to his senses and sought a house in the nearest metropolis, which turned out to be Washington, DC.

The narrow Federal town house on Potomac Street in Georgetown was ideal—intimate drawing rooms on the main floor; dining room, kitchen, and garden on the bottom; and a splendid master suite on top. Since he was also transitioning careers from banker to bookseller, the layout lent itself to a sort of *Gosford Park* style of entertaining where he and clients could leaf through first-edition manuscripts pulled off the loaded bookshelves in the living room while dinner was being prepared and then served—out of sight—below.

Langham intuitively began with an autumnal palette: golden apricot, burnt sugar, oatmeal, scarlet, eggplant, and moss green. A sort of tweedy glamour followed by way of juxtaposing wide-wale linen velvet with heavy silk taffeta, Bernard Thorp tree-of-life linen next to waxed leathers. Good antiques from Gerald Bland in New York were reused and mixed with local finds and family heirlooms. Just walking through the front door feels like making a civilized entrance; regrettably many houses today forgo the tiny vestibule hall so common in turn-of-the-century city architecture. Here the vestibule is treated with charming wallpaper and good lighting—a spot to drop an umbrella and maybe even take off snowy boots. A night door allows the vestibule to be closed off after visiting hours and is reopened to let in light during the day. The results are a paean to a bygone era—brandies in the drawing room, a book in your lap, and a dog curled up at your feet.

A historic tone is set in the entry's vestibule using Adelphi's arsenic-green nineteenth-century document wallpaper and an antique American bell-jar lantern. An unfortunately positioned radiator, disguised in lattice and outfitted with a slate top, cleverly passes as an entrance hall console and is further legitimized by a chunky William Kent-style mirror hanging above. Mounted antlers riff on Virginia's sporting heritage.

Haunted by Evangeline Bruce's Georgetown drawing room ("I still dream about her apricot walls"), Langham chose a similar golden hue for this room. Since the town house is horizontally challenged a clear mirror on either side of the fireplace trickily expands the dimensions. A smattering of good English antiques and inherited hand-me-downs are artfully mixed. A well-proportioned coffee table from Ikea even holds its own in the pastiche.

ABOVE: The ritual of lighting candles every night is a lost one, but here on special evenings, with the sconces and fireplace ablaze, the drawing room glows deep amber. OPPOSITE: The client suggested some flounce at the windows, and he got it. Heavy silk festoon curtains with aubergine wool fringe (made in Georgetown by a hard-to-book seamstress whom Langham tirelessly pursued) drop all the way to the floor. "Hoisting them back up requires two people!" The faded Oushak is actually a brilliant reproduction found through a dealer in Charlottesville.

Rudimentary bookcases made of plywood and painted white are loaded with beloved titles, which are often sold right off the shelf! A moody James River painting over the mantel weights the room with Virginia's important role in American history, while a contemporary red leather slipper chair counterbalances with a bit of zip.

The drawing room palette is reversed in the downstairs dining room. Here a rich scarlet takes the lead across crewel curtains whose final lining (the fabric that faces the outside) is a vivid red. Even though one of the openings is actually a door leading to the back garden, it is treated in an identical fashion to maintain symmetry—with Gothic pelmets and brass holdbacks. Inherited Regency chairs with leather seat cushions surround the table like well-dressed soldiers. Langham embraced the low ceilings by staining the walls a match-strike color, which actually expands the room and "feels dramatic like the midnight sky."

ABOVE: A civilized master suite on the top floor is almost like a second library. Turquoise upholstered walls with ribbon-band boxing (a trick for outlining walls without crown moldings) and a Greek-key bull's-eye mirror are backdrop for the handsome, suede-upholstered bed. The patchwork quilt was a last-minute find, spotted on the last day of installation in the window of Georgetown's Marston Luce Antiques. "Sometimes it's that last un-thought-of detail that *makes* the composition!" **OPPOSITE:** The twelve-drawer, green-slate-topped chest found in England remains one of Langham's all-time favorite pieces. A heavy linen shade coupled with floor-to-ceiling Raoul Fabric curtains and a soft, folded valence not only muffles street noise but also ensures total blackout in the case of a bad bout of katzenjammer.

BARN AGAIN

Langham explains his relationship with a lifelong friend turned client, "We got married in the middle of a field when we were six years old. Gorgeous food and flowers. It was the social event of the season!" Other than planning their wedding, the pair got up to a myriad of mischief growing up in Brewton, Alabama, where you had to make your own fun. Their paths eventually led them both to the Northeast, where Langham made his mark in design and his best friend worked her way up the corporate ladder to become the CEO of several Fortune 500 companies. When she landed a job overseeing an operation based in Pennsylvania, she and her (official) husband packed up the family and moved from Manhattan to a quaint Pennsylvania Dutch stone house smack in the middle of Amish country.

Set on twenty-five undulating acres with a winding creek, the property was vast. She felt not unlike Eva Gabor on *Green Acres* so she placed a lifeline call to her pal to come to the rescue. The main house would require massive renovation, so in the meantime she and Langham focused on sprucing up one of the outbuildings, an old tobacco barn, to eventually be used as a summerhouse for guests but, more immediately, as a temporary campsite for her family while enduring construction. A cavernous split-timber and plaster structure built in the early 1900s, the barn still had dirt floors and curing leaves. Austin architect John Miller Mayfield was brought on board to scheme out a rustically refined, four-bedroom plan. For her part, the client was hesitant to go "full barn" and urged her designers to focus on luxury.

As the building morphed into a lavish retreat, simultaneously the spirit of Pennsylvania was casting an enchanted spell over Langham and his client, and they dove deeper into the local aesthetic. Langham hit nearby shops for quilts and cutting boards. He hired local craftsmen to make rustic furniture. They drove to Brimfield—the famed antique show in Massachusetts—and loaded up a truck. He and Mayfield harvested local wood for all the floors. "The project came together and was sort of much more than any of us imagined," Langham recalls. "It's a good thing, too, because the main house took three and half years to renovate!" They even added another structure to the property, a gloriously folksy Palladian folly situated at one end of the swimming pool, which Langham likes to tease would be the ideal spot to renew their vows.

The transformation from a dirt-floored, dusty tobacco barn into a sumptuous, rustic retreat is a feat of spatial planning. The architect John Miller Mayfield conceived a thoughtful design, which has a central staircase bisecting the barn, delineating different living zones, and becoming the barn's chief focal point. Here, the German folk-style balustrade on the mezzanine level acts like a decorative crown for the entrance hall.

Pennsylvania stone marries well
with creosote-painted barn boards
and oxblood mullions. The house
mascot, a gilded grasshopper
inspired by the legendary golden
weathervane at Boston's Faneuil
Hall, surveys all from his perch atop
the barn's cupola

The barn's structural timber was reclaimed from nearby dilapidated buildings, and its walls are made with tinted, polished plaster. Back-to-back sofas and overstuffed Langham & Company club chairs wear Schumacher-printed linen and are accessorized with down-stuffed throw pillows in alternating red and beige buffalo checks. Since the enormous windows required yards of fabric, Langham chose inexpensive burlap found at an Amish market and had it edged with a made-to-order braid. Painted wooden pelmets dress up the humble material.

OPPOSITE: A wheel-base chandelier anchors the dining area and by night, its red-lined lampshades cast a rosy glow. Chairs covered in supple, pale green hides soften a Pennsylvania Dutch farm table. **ABOVE:** The client decided she needed a break from brown wood so Langham had the staircase wallboards painted in several tones of Prussian-blue milk paint and sanded through.

ABOVE: A colloquial Pennsylvania Dutch painted detail in the chimney's inglenook, which is tucked in under the staircase next to the kitchen. OPPOSITE: Langham had the vintage Garland range reconditioned and enameled green. An old-fashioned tile backsplash is installed along the entire stove wall. Pots and pans hang from hooks off the rafters, and a giant porcelain rooster reminds everyone, needlessly, that they are in a country kitchen. Cabinets with scalloped trim were painted pomegranate, a color that feels just right in the country.

ABOVE: The staircase, a geometric feat of engineering, originates in the basement and winds its way up to the barn's lookout cupola. Here, a bridge leads to bedrooms on either side with a shared bathroom in between. **OPPOSITE:** Langham made the enormous, early American Paul Bunyan bed and coated it with a wash of green milk paint. Since the bed is high off the ground, wall brackets were installed on either side of it instead of bedside tables, which would have been too low. Luxurious ivory wool and linen crewel curtains hang from a quilted, bowfront pelmet edged with a small linen loop.

PREVIOUS SPREAD: Rusticated stone columns and a series of classic pediments conjure a Palladian temple nestled among tall trees. Langham plays up the folly's symmetry by positioning the dining table on an axis with the center of the pool. The mirror over the fireplace repeats the oval shape of the doors and becomes a tertiary architectural element. Canvas curtains installed between upright columns glide across iron poles to create an enclosed room.

RIGHT: Each wing of the pool house has a cozy seating area featuring oversize, wood-framed furniture, aqua buttoned-mattress cushions, and plenty of Turkish throw pillows. On a shopping trip through Connecticut, Langham returned with an early American tole lantern, which flickers romantically at night.

GEORGIAN ON MY MIND

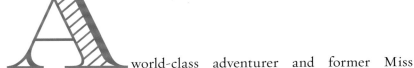

A world-class adventurer and former Miss Mississippi, the homeowner had globetrotted to the outmost corners of the Earth, but the region closest to her heart still remained the Deep South. When she and her husband decided to build their dream dwelling on an empty parcel in Jackson, she had an idea of what it ought to look like: a commanding Irish manor house with well-bred rooms and piles of Southern charm. She hired seasoned Mississippi architect Lewis Graeber III, who took her idea to the next level, drafting up an eighteenth-century, scored-stucco Georgian triumph. Along the way, Graeber recommended his frequent collaborator—Langham—to realize the interiors. It was a match made in Mississippi.

Besides being crazy about the great houses of Europe, the homeowner, Graeber, and Langham shared a specific kind of Southern reverence for home and hospitality and . . . fried chicken. They rolled up their sleeves and began what would take almost three years to complete. For his part, Langham was determined to create the kind of proper European rooms that he and the client were inspired by, but with the weight lifted. To that end, he adhered to an uncharacteristically leaner look, which in many ways is more challenging because every silhouette counts. "We wanted it to be clean, but luxuriously so," the decorator says, "which meant a rigorous edit of the best of everything." The rosy palette swung between warm pink in the living room and bold crimson in the entrance hall, turning up again as crushed azalea in the garden room.

After patiently enduring years of construction, dust, and decisions, with the furniture at last in position, the art hung and the pillows fluffed, architect, decorator, and client were finally able to take a collective bow for their masterpiece: a Southern ode to Irish grace. As the romantic poet John Keats once wrote, "A thing of beauty is a joy forever." And for this winsome house, that sentiment is quite apt.

A graceful Irish Georgian leaded-glass transom sits atop obsidian-lacquered night doors which, when opened, allow for an enfilade vista straight from the entry vestibule through the pink drawing room and ending at the garden's domed conservatory.

ABOVE: The limestone entry-hall floor is paved with a central compass pointing to four wall murals depicting the continents in which the client had spent time. An exuberant arrangement of peppermint camellias echoes the entry vestibule's dramatic crimson splash. **OPPOSITE:** "We wanted the flourish, color, and scale of European houses, but more tailored." An overscale and voluptuous ivory sofa trimmed in bullion fringe sits underneath a monumental, romantic English landscape.

With an enormous Palladian window and hefty plaster frieze, the barrel-vaulted living room's strong architecture is softened by warm walls and overstuffed upholstery. An array of seating includes two Irish Gainsborough chairs dressed in watermelon and grass, three Langham & Company notched-back club chairs in a classic Brunschwig & Fils chintz, and a silk velvet pouf nicknamed "the tuffet" centrally positioned in front of the exquisite English mantelpiece. The Oushak's delicate palette drove the room's colors, especially the shadow-striped walls that Langham says, "have an incredible glow, which captivates everyone at first sight."

Gilded plaster reliefs are centered above twin pediment cabinets, designed by architect Lewis Graeber III for the purpose of showcasing a robust collection of Irish Belleek porcelain. Hepplewhite wheel-back chairs with saffron-colored Fortuny seats stand alert in the living room until called for dinner party duty in the dining room.

OPPOSITE: Swaths of pink and ivory silk provide a glamorously chic enfilade view from the garden room toward the living room. Langham gilded a pair of antique torchères, which are the ideal height for a statement-making spray of magnolia arranged in giant urns. **ABOVE:** The tented garden room has a zingy palette and is filled with bespoke Langham & Company iron furniture. Here, the settee has a laser-cut, scalloped apron and mattress-style cushion covered in shocking azalea pink.

Cocktail parties usually start with mint juleps served in the garden room and then migrate toward the living or dining room for supper. White Alabama and Absolute black marble pave the floor while black and off-white canvas tents the ceiling. Walls and windows are hung with opaque ivory cotton whose obsidian cuffs frame the view.

Despite the lushness of coffee-bean-colored walls, the dining room remains luxuriously spare due in part to a sleek mirrored trumeau whose clean lines melt into the fireplace's Sienna marble bolection. Mismatched English porcelain circles a pair of gilt-wood sconces. A set (one is out of frame) of deep L-shaped banquettes covered in grass-green velvet carves out the corners.

OPPOSITE: Monogrammed slipcovers network with mature Hepplewhite chairs lightening the mood around the Regency table. A chinoiserie valence, attached to a serpentine gilded pelmet, frames the oversize window. ABOVE: A collection of sterling silver goblets pairs perfectly with acid-green heraldic china. The rusted patina of a marble-topped iron console adds an unexpected layer of texture.

ABOVE: The bedside commode's exquisite marquetry inlay of Diana the Huntress reminded Langham of the outdoorsy lady of the house. Brown and white fabric for bed hangings and window curtains are dyed pale cantaloupe to connect with a hushed apricot ceiling.
OPPOSITE: Crenelated gothic pelmets crown the bed and windows. Aquamarine silk fabric lines the interior bed canopy, and walls are glazed pearl.

A Bedroom and a Ballroom

Summoned by a recently divorced pal to decorate her bachelorette residence on Central Park South at the Gainsborough Studios building, Langham committed to the task, declaring it to be one of his top five apartments in all of New York: "It's got ideal dimensions."

Small yet admirably scaled, the space boasts an extraordinary double-height living room with epic park views and frosty Northern light. Architect Rob Shutler was hired to improve the closet and bathroom configuration, as well as redirect the staircase to elegantly turn into the middle of the living room. Classical elements like dentil moldings, pediments, and columns were added while being careful not to distract from the treetop view of the park in all four seasons.

The client, a philanthropist with a full-tilt social schedule, had a clear vision: simplicity and serenity. She encouraged Langham to lean into a tailored Bohemian look rather than Upper East Side formality; items on the wish list included oversize daybeds in lieu of traditional sofas, the color lilac, and a pared-down edit of every single item coming in the door from her previous apartment.

Langham responded thoughtfully with a monochromatic palette (a departure for the decorator known for exuberant color) that allowed Central Park to be the first gasp and the interiors, the second: "I wanted to harness the colors of the sky on a cloudy day: gray, amethyst, aubergine, oyster, iron, pearl, lightning, charcoal." Since the palette was hushed, texture would be critical; steel and glass, silk and mohair, warm wood and sparkling mirror.

Langham sought out shapes that would engage with all the negative space, insisting, "Every silhouette counts in a volumetric room!" Making the brutal cut were an important gilded Régence commode, Jacob oval-back chairs, and a pair of fruitwood Russian bergères with griffin arm supports. Overall, the effect is of a glamorous, icy aerie warmed up by a culled collection of good art and antiques—the ideal backdrop for a simple dinner by the fire or cocktails for sixty. As Langham loves to exclaim about the bedroom and ballroom apartment, "Really! What more do you need?"

Ensconced in shades of black mink, the entrance hall's striéd plaster walls and lead-crystal console from Baccarat cue icy glamour while a pair of walnut Jacob oval-back chairs, limestone floors, and an English portrait of a certain Lady Fairfax portend a collector's eye for antiquity. The modern Tony Duquette starburst light fixture provides a sleek exclamation point.

"I interviewed twenty-five shades of pale gray for the walls . . . testing every color in every light," Langham says. Matte Revere Pewter (HC-172) by Benjamin Moore won, and the woodwork was picked out in glossy white. Frosty rock-crystal sconces and Lucite side tables add subtle sparkle, allowing a marble bust of Hercules (that once belonged to Bill Blass) to commandeer the room from his perch atop a Régence commode while a pair of Russian fruitwood bergères lyrically carves out the negative space.

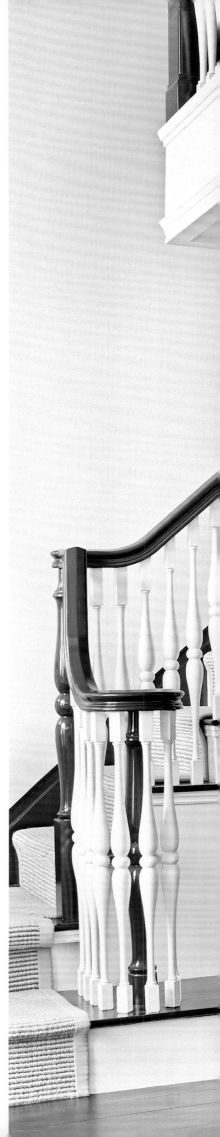

ABOVE: In a monochromatic room, a variety of texture is tantamount to success. A soft gray saddle-stitched leather banquette curves around Julian Chichester's lacquered linen Dakota table with its reflective nickel base. Mirror panels cleverly disguise a structural column, and a Richard Serra painting activates the matte gray wall above. **RIGHT:** "The apartment is all living room," Langham says. "You can have sixty over for cocktails, so a bar tucked under the stairs is an inspired use of space." With paneled cabinetry painted the same hue as the entrance hall, the bar echoes classic architectural elements found throughout the apartment, but is meant to recede. Humble sisal matting runs up the stairs and covers the mezzanine gallery floor.

OPPOSITE: *Purple Thunder* by Cleve Gray and a ten-foot-long sofa establish the secondary seating area under the gallery. Dark and light chairs duel across the coffee table, and an ottoman upholstered in snow-leopard silk velvet delineates the two sides of the room.
ABOVE: The minstrel gallery, which doubles as a library, runs along the west side of the living room's perfect thirty-foot-square footprint, providing a de facto gang plank to catch the view outside as well as down below.

Langham's primary intention was to celebrate the sweeping views up Central Park. With uncharacteristic restraint, the decorator's palette hews toward the gray scale, and the furniture and art are rigorously edited. An extra-tall trumeau mirror above the fireplace emphasizes verticality while two oversize chaises longues covered in soft angora mohair visually expand the space.

A nod to 1930s New York glamour, the bedroom's luxurious silk wool Berber carpet softens the floor, and amethyst printed-linen fabric covers the walls, cushions the headboard, and pulls across the wall of south-facing windows for total blackout. The four-poster iron bed is topped with icy crystal finials, and a pair of mohair club chairs sits on either side of the fireplace.

POMP AND CIRCUMSTANCE

It was fate that tossed the decorator and his clients together some twenty years ago. At the time, Langham was deployed on a real estate mission to Bronxville, New York, by another client looking for his seal of approval on a purchase. Upon arrival at the destination in question, the lady of the house—whom he noticed staring as if trying to recall him from some previous exchange—led Langham through its rooms and gardens. Suddenly she turned and said, "Wait a minute, are you Keith of Richard Keith Langham? I've been meaning to call you for weeks!" Her husband had a dog-eared copy of *New York* magazine sitting on the beside table—with Langham's picture in it—and every night for the past month, he would remind his wife to make contact with the designer. And, without ever having picked up the telephone, there he was standing in her living room.

The relationship seemed to be written in the stars. In fact, she wound up selling her house to Langham's client and, to her husband's infinite delight, appointed him decorator on their new sprawling estate, called Chelmsford, in Greenwich, Connecticut. Built around 1914 as a stately yet nonetheless modest house, McKim, Mead & White (arguably *the* architectural firm of its era) oversaw its considerable expansion. Langham remembers being dumbstruck driving up the sinuous, half-mile long approach and glimpsing this great clapboard and stone house with canted wings on either side: "It was like a small hotel."

First things first, Langham whisked his new friend to London, where they spent several days negotiating the purchase of a pair of drop-dead carpets and good English antiques. A packed container was shipped back to New York, and the decorations began in earnest. Work orders were placed with Langham's favorite cut-to-measure rug company in Italy, and a beloved Bailey & Griffin chintz (a pattern Langham has held in his mind since he was seven years old and noticed it covering *everything* in the bedroom of a hometown doyenne) was recolored in Philadelphia and a tea-stained ground added. Langham worked round the clock with his team of artisans and upholsterers perfecting each and every nuance of lacquered and stippled wall, curtain pleat, and tufted ottoman. Tone for tone, the decorations echo the turn-of-the-century architecture in a splendid show of pageantry.

The balustrade makes a lyrical spiral around the thirty-foot-square entrance hall. A pair of intricately painted chairs and pedestal table—copied from an original Regency dining table in dimensions more suitable to the house—sit atop a rare Turkish Ghiordes carpet. A bronze and gilt Regency hall lantern, whose inside roof Langham painted a bright claret "to give it some verve," was found in London.

PRECEDING SPREAD: The living room reaches back in time to the 1920s, the original era of the house, without compromising on modern conveniences. Ten-foot-long, back-to-back lolling sofas are covered in rich linen velvet—a go-to fabric because it looks better with wear unlike a silk velvet, which bruises too easily. The bouclé carpet, woven in Pennsylvania, combines different sized loops of wool that contribute to its lively texture. Occasional chairs are covered in rich amethyst satin. Says the designer, "I always like a dose of glamour to dress up a fancy room." **ABOVE:** To emphasize their gilt-wood backplates, crystal drop sconces were rewired with elongated fifteen-inch candles and wear Tiffany-blue pleated shades. **OPPOSITE:** An elliptical Adam-style border mirror was designed to fit the expansive chimney breast. Langham & Company notched-back club chairs are covered in a favorite Bailey & Griffin chintz that Langham had recolored to suit the room.

RIGHT: Decorative painter Judy Mulligan glazed original plaster walls Prussian blue and varnished them repeatedly, building layers of "midnight-colored waves shimmering in the moonlight." The bowed banquette, whose skirt falls straight from button tufting, hugs the curve of the wall. A mercury-glass screen reflects light back into the room, and an enormous painting from John Rosselli in New York commands the grouping.

FOLLOWING SPREAD: The nineteenth-century Bessarabian carpet and half halo of ivory curtains accentuate the dining room's subtle palette. Good Georgian dining chairs are dressed in honeydew-striped cotton satin slipcovers.

ABOVE: When asked, the decorator will happily set the table. Here, antique Coalport china, green glass, and sterling silver circle a centerpiece of peach-colored roses and thirty-inch tapers. **OPPOSITE:** The elaborate plaster crown molding is highlighted in rich cream, while vivid pink-grapefruit walls energize the quiet palette and look marvelous at night. A six-legged, English Regency server of crotch mahogany sits below an eighteenth-century Dutch painting from Gerald Bland.

Yards of black and cream neo-classical toile de Jouy lined with apple-green silk satin, complete with smocked valence and blocked fringe, are suspended from the ceiling to create a formidable canopy bed. Sublime apple-green walls are a degree paler in value than the interior panels of the bed hangings.

OPPOSITE: The chimney breast is painted to look like Spanish Negro Marquina and Italian Calacatta Gold marble. An alabaster mantel clock, Wedgewood plates, and whimsical forged-iron wall lights support the black and white motif. ABOVE: A Pierre-Auguste Renoir oil painting crowns the ebonized *bureau plat* with a *cartonniére*, built by Frederick P. Victoria & Sons. Caned-back French armchairs are dressed in apple-green quilted cotton.

SINCE I FELL FOR YOU

The East Memphis estate on which this house stands belonged to chart-topping, country singer Charlie Rich. Even though Rich was from Arkansas, his mark was made at Sun Records and he always called Memphis home. When Langham's clients acquired the Rich property it had been subdivided into several bucolic parcels, which meant ground-up construction was required. Architect Lewis Graeber III was brought on board to design in the type of Acadian vernacular for which he is sought after, which includes Colonial Caribbean louvered shutters, salvaged cypress boards, and plenty of tall French doors and breezy galleries. Similarly, Langham drew inspiration for the interiors from a deep well of experience spent below the Mason-Dixon line. "Many cities in the South hold tight to the rituals of previous generations, and Memphis is one of them," Langham says. "The place is a bastion of good manners . . . people just have an innate knowledge of the right way to do things."

To start, the decorator established a sense of suitability and ease throughout the house; quiet corners with deep club chairs for reading, games tables for lively rounds of bridge, and cozy spots for watching the news. It being the South, living rooms spill onto verandas for indoor/outdoor entertaining plus seating is scaled up for luncheons and dinner parties. Rooms were cast in a harmonious blend of vivid and neutral hues—burnt orange, Chinese red, persimmon, salmon, parchment, taupe, aquamarine, spearmint, and jade. And perhaps most importantly, compositions arranged with sentimental art and objects imbued the young house with a rich personal story. As Langham likes to say, "Homeowners' things lend depth, a we've-always-been-here look." While the husband was a fourth-generation Tennessee man, the wife, with whom Langham had collaborated previously, was new to Memphis and not quite sure whether this house would be her primary residence.

Langham and Graeber, who had worked together many times and communicated in a creative shorthand, delivered the couple a temple of elegance and propriety that looked as if it had been there forever. Indeed, their client fell head over heels for her new house as well as for Memphis, and with a broad smile now refers to both as home.

A substantial Régence console and moody landscape painting, both picked up in New Orleans, establish a Continental tone in the entrance hall. The lantern's glass is replaced with panels of stretched pongee silk to diffuse the glare of bare bulbs. Plastered brick and a stone floor are warmed by pomegranate-colored wool challis at the window and a wool velvet carpet running up the stairs.

In order to create a private Eden in the heart of a residential neighborhood, the house was purposefully inverted so that the public rooms open on to an interior courtyard with a perimeter wall encircling the property. Blue-green shutters, whose color threads throughout the interiors, offset creamy stucco walls.

ABOVE: Langham chose a parchment color for the central core and painted smaller vestibules, which punctuate the galleries that run along either side of the house, in darker tones. **OPPOSITE:** Adhering to tradition, the living room is as polite as can be, although cheeky eruptions of color, like the Régence armchair covered in disruptive peacock-blue velvet, keep the room from being uptight. The painting is by Irish abstract expressionist Michael Madigan.

RIGHT: "Even though there's a lot of square footage, this house feels wonderful to move through," Langham says. "It leads you down these meandering halls through dark vestibules and into light-filled spaces." Indeed, the living room, with fixed louvered panels on both sides, is a bright open space thanks to the light streaming in from gallery windows on each side. Back-to-back sofas face matching fireplaces—this view shows a period Régence mirror. **FOLLOWING SPREAD:** Often one element will galvanize an entire room. In this case, the client's inherited Japanese screen inspired Langham to canvas the dining room walls in squares of colored silk intermittently gold leafed with a gestural motif. Even the homeowner was surprised, stating, "In four houses, this screen has never looked as good as it does against patchwork!" Of the eight chairs around the custom walnut table, only one is original. Plucked out of a junk shop in Atlanta, the chair was so good-looking and comfortable that Langham had nine copies whipped up and covered in coral leather with silk gingham outside backs.

"Despite what they look like, hodgepodge rooms require effort!" the decorator laughs. A Breck-style sofa in camel mohair situates the library while an assortment of cozy chairs in damask, paisley, and red leather circle round. The lacquered desk topped with a leather blotter insert is from John Boone in New York. The bouillotte lamp finished with a sang-de-boeuf-painted metal shade is marvelously off color from the oxblood Christopher Spitzmiller lamps on either side of the sofa. But it's the Oushak carpet, with its rare coloration, that makes everyone swoon.

ABOVE: A round dining table sits at one end of the family room in the bay window niche. Mullions are painted milk chocolate, which migrates onto the ceiling as well. OPPOSITE: A vermilion linen wallcovering and an oversize wool hooked carpet animate the long, narrow family room. A printed tree-of-life pattern is scattered across upholstery and curtains, while the ten-foot-long sofa, dressed in decadent teal linen velvet, is planted in the center. A games table for weekly bridge tournaments tucks into the bay window at the far end of the room.

ABOVE: The client, an avid horticulturist, takes pleasure in the many pocket gardens that hug outward-facing rooms.
OPPOSITE: Langham has expressed an aversion to generic white kitchens; here, buoyant colors, such as Chinese red and pale turquoise, keep the mood cheerful. Hand-painted tiles line the enormous stove niche contributing to the cheery temperament. Gingham checks, piped in chocolate, cover the pelmet above the sink as well as the flounced cushions on kitchen stool seats.

The outside world retreats in the master bedroom; walls are hung with a printed Brunschwig fabric and the tray ceiling is painted a clear aquamarine. Old-fashioned bowfront valences with diamond smocking and curtains are sumptuous with ivory satin and bright peacock fringe.

ABOVE: The curve of the apple-green French headboard mimics the serpentine shape of the bedside table. Lighting is generated from two sources: above the shoulder for reading or diffused illumination from the turquoise table lamp. **OPPOSITE:** "The bathroom is a dream!" Polished porcelain floor tiles and glazed sherbet woodwork amp up glamour. Semi-sheer linen damask curtains pull across the length of the window, blurring the garden view. A gorgeous Louis XVI fauteuil receives fluffy stacks of towels when needed.

INTO THE WOODS

Explaining the point of this hidden kingdom rising up like a mirage in the middle of a thicket of pines, on the edge of a gurgling creek in the middle of nowhere, Langham humorously offers, "It's a refuge from the bustling metropolis of Hattiesburg, Mississippi!" Besides solitude, there is sport. Longleaf Plantation is a hallowed lodge situated on four thousand acres devoted to the gentlemanly pursuits of catching fowl, fin, and game. If neither hunting nor fishing is your cup of bourbon, then perhaps dining on freshly prepared quail with homemade fig preserves or fried catfish and hushpuppies might be.

Langham and his frequent collaborator, esteemed architect Lewis Graeber III, had previously renovated and decorated the family's beloved primary residence a half hour up the road, so naturally the two were summoned once again. The clients specifically wanted to build a refined yet woodsy weekend house; a cozy retreat where they could not only spend a night alone under the stars but also organize grand affairs from family weddings to reunions. Under the direction of Graeber, local builder Adam Hodges and his all-star team of woodworkers amassed an impressive array of indigenous materials, such as wide yellow pine for floorboards and rough-cut cypress for beams and paneling, as well as plenty of roots, vines, and bark for decorative elements. Even though the materials were primitive, the actual construction realized the finer points of a proper house showcasing charming details like the pierced splat balusters zigzagging up three flights of stairs and mosaic twig panels inset into chimney breasts. The sheer amount of finesse involved in the labor is astonishing, especially in the living room, where hand-chinked horizontal logs soar upward to clerestory windows and a hipped roof.

For his part, Langham concocted an alpine base note, layering textures such as corduroy, tartan, burlap, and leather with sheepskin and beaver. Good English antiques contributed a civilized note and, scouring all the county's local junk shops and thrift stores for small treasures, Langham masterfully blended the fine with the humble. Approaching the house—from a winding red-dirt road lined with magnolias and oaks—feels like the beginning of a Grimms' fairy tale, "Once upon a time, in a great big house in the middle of the woods . . ."

Cleverly suspended from a single support, not one but three lanterns descend in size, illuminating the shaft of the three-story stairwell. Horizontal wall boards and pierced, splat-style balusters are painted in creosote black and barn red.

OPPOSITE: Rough-cut beams and boards create informal paneling that Langham appoints with art as well as three-dimensional curiosities. A locally made Adirondack-style chair gets covered in a striped wool rug fragment. **ABOVE:** An alpine plotline unfolds in the living room. An enormous thirty-foot-square hooked rug shares the same folksy sensibility as the curtains, whose rectangles of burlap are overlock-stitched with red yarn. Bronze curtain rods are capped with articulated castings of pinecones.

ABOVE: Organic bent-root chairs were purchased at Olympia, London's vast art and antiques fair. The carved wood doe locks eyes with a sleek stag across the room. **OPPOSITE:** Large fragments of kilims were used to upholster the locally made, two-sided twig-and-root settee, whose back faces toward another small seating area. Beyond the carved stag, through the bay windows, is a waterfall whose rushing water is like an ambient soundtrack.

Locally harvested wood creates
warmth and intimacy throughout
the residence. Straight-back
leather chairs mingle with the
rounded English Windsor variety
down the length of the sixteen-
foot-long dining table. A pair of
English banquet-hall chandeliers
illuminates the scene.

OPPOSITE: A warm embrace: creosote walls meet a cypress beam-and-board ceiling while an area rug, channeling a hand-knit sweater, reaches practically to the corners of the room. The colossal four-poster bed, cutting a luxe-folk silhouette, wears a patchwork quilt, gingham ruffled pillows, and a raccoon blanket. ABOVE: A diversity of woodland creatures inhabits the master bedroom including ceramic figurines and bronze owl andirons foraged on "junktiquing" trips, but a Swiss painting of twin fawns against an umber sky steals the scene. Tone-on-tone crewel curtains have a diamond-medallion pattern and are trimmed with espresso fringe. Twig marquetry caps the bowed curtain valence, riffing on the inset panel at the fireplace.

A SUNNY DISPOSITION

About the kaleidoscopic wonderland he created for his clients, Langham explains, "They jokingly refer to it as the 'Fun House.'" The couple, whose main residence in Connecticut is a vast and proper affair, was shopping for a winter retreat in Palm Beach where they could relax the formality a bit. Almost immediately, they met the one: a sophisticated 1950s Regency that boasted a twenty-five-foot-tall manicured ficus hedge cloaking the house in privacy. The best feature, however, of this exceptional property was by far its location. With the Atlantic two blocks away and Worth Avenue five blocks away, biking and walking would soon replace driving. In effect, the house was a hidden, seaside oasis in the heart of Palm Beach.

Funnily enough, on the morning of Langham's interview with the client in New York, he had an appointment with an antiques dealer. There, he spied a pair of the most gloriously Floridian-looking seahorse-and-coral sconces that seemed tailor-made for the house. It was as if the decorating gods were conspiring to make things work out. He took a sconce off the wall to show his potential client. She quickly signed off on not only Langham but also the seahorses as well: "We *have* to have them!"

The project soared, partially due to his client's ability to communicate precisely what she wanted—"a lighthearted, sunny house"—but also to the trust she bestowed on Langham to get her there. He decided that color would be the vehicle in which to meet that end. Once that was decided, the floodgates opened; the client's first dictate, after the seahorse sconces, was to paint the front door a glossy tangerine and to lacquer the entrance hall lime green. "That really got the ball rolling!" Langham laughs. Color was skillfully measured—in one room pale aqua and coral are the main course and in another watermelon and ice blue are a dollop on top. The result is a balanced meal that feels like just enough. Besides waging his cheer campaign on the interiors, Langham also redesigned the exterior patio, transforming a bleak uncovered space with zero architecture into a glamorous, tented poolside pavilion where the family truly whiles away their days and nights. The decorator, enthusiastic about this particular job and client, notes, "We designed the perfect Palm Beach playground!"

The client wanted a lime-green lacquered entrance hall and after nine coats of painting and sanding, she got it! White marble floor tiles laid out with black cabochons further establish Palm Beach glamour. The pagoda lantern and Venetian torchère are painted matte white to flatter the gloss.

The living room is restrained yet still animated. Dollops of clear vibrant color appear here and there; vermicelli quilted cotton pops on a curved daybed tucked into the alcove of a bow window, duck's-egg blue covers a bergére, and lime-green suede freshens up oval back Italian arm chairs. Simple white scrim curtains and chalky grass-cloth walls keep the room ethereal.

OPPOSITE: Average-height ceilings are lifted by glassy, sky-blue lacquer. A Langham & Fine Indian dhurrie rug with a palmette pattern gives the room lyrical geometry, and the watermelon-colored linen velvet sofa provides a cheerful exclamation point. ABOVE: Curious palm-tree sconces were scored on South Dixie Highway and reimagined with two coats of white gesso. The gilt-wood faux-bamboo overmantel mirror is English Regency. Three small watercolor animals demand a closer look.

ABOVE: The seahorse-and-coral sconces were a lucky find at a New York antiques dealer moments before Langham met his client for the first time. He took one out on approval, brought it to the meeting, and the rest is history. Heavy, coral linen curtains with a running dog border hang from a pagoda-shaped pelmet finished at the corners with gilded tinker bells. **OPPOSITE:** The dining room was a nondescript affair until Langham hired a pair of Parisian artisans to tent the ceiling in a trompe-l'oeil effect called *paraplui*, "umbrella" in French. With pale aqua walls and a coral-and-white canvas ceiling, the dining room was at once transformed into a fantasy. Looped-back Frances Elkins chairs contrast with the ebonized pedestal table. A crystal chandelier is hung thirty inches from the tabletop to ensure it is included in the conversation.

LEFT: Bedroom walls hung with Scalamandré lime-green silk paisley embrace a dusty-lavender ceiling and a lush, amethyst silk-bamboo carpet from Stark. The star of the show, however, is the elaborately carved Victor & Sons nine-foot-tall four-poster bed with apple-green silk, tented ceiling, and white leather headboard. ABOVE: Ethereal ombréd linen curtains from Osborne & Little draw attention to the upstairs sitting room. A chunky parson's-style coffee table wrapped in vegetable-dyed stingray skins sits on top of a dotted carpet from Portugal.

Henri Bendel-esque chocolate-and-ivory-striped upholstery sets a crisp tone in the tented poolside pavilion where the family spends most of their time. "The patio, previously an uncovered affair, has ultimately become the focal point of the house," says Langham, who bolstered the architecture by positioning painted, cast-iron columns around the tent's perimeter and a mother-of-pearl coping around the swimming pool's waterline for effervescent sparkle.

A Home at the End of the World

Besides the remote setting on eighty acres of wild, protected pasture, this summer retreat is also perched on the pristine Miles River (a freshwater tributary for Maryland's Eastern Bay, which ultimately flows into the Chesapeake), providing a kind of view to eternity. It's no surprise then that the homeowners christened their 1920s white clapboard house Miles-A-Way and use it, alongside their dogs and occasional houseguests, for tuning out the world and reconnecting with the land and waterways.

After decades of friendship with their decorator, the pair knew Langham would be able to exactly interpret what they meant by their directive, "We want it to feel like a trip to grandmother's." Indeed, Langham rolled up his sleeves and set a course bound for tradition and comfort: "This house recognizes the past, but it also has every modern creature comfort at arm's reach." Colors were picked from the palette of an Eastern Shore summer: garden tomato bisque; pale lettuce and cucumber; butter yellow; sky, slate, and admiral's blue. Maritime influences prevailed including nautical flags, lanterns on pulleys, and a Gracie mural washed in indigo, depicting the landmarks of the closest town, Saint Michaels. The homeowners wanted a garden room, so a small wing was added to the house. Inspired by the Regency exoticism of the Royal Pavilion in Brighton and the garden club–esque fretwork of a room in Sister Parish's house in Dark Harbor, Maine, Langham dreamed up a clever "haute MawMaw" space, where his clients wound up spending the majority of their time, especially for drinks at sunset. "Miles-A-Way really lives up to its name," Langham says. "Listening to birdsong and water lapping the shore, you feel positively renewed."

A nineteenth-century French lantern, suspended between the first and second floors, allows close-up inspection of finely detailed bronze ropes and pulleys.

RIGHT: A clipped allée of boxwood leads to the river-facing front door. Built in the 1920s, the rambling exterior clapboard is painted a historic crisp white with minty shutters. FOLLOWING SPREAD: Like many grand houses situated on the water, all perspectives are focused on the horizon. Here, the front door is often kept open for the warm summer cross-breeze. Dark wood and butter-yellow walls historically situate the house. The cotton Agra carpet was found in New York.

PRECEDING SPREAD: The living room runs from the front of the house to the back and is divided into three seating groups, each anchored by cheerful, paisley linen. Langham sampled several colors off the green-blue scale, from deep mint to pale honeydew, before finally settling on a warm-toned aquamarine for the walls. **OPPOSITE:** An array of ceramic and bronze figurines lands on top of and inside a handsome secretary. **ABOVE:** Paintings of the USS *Macedonian* on turbulent seas by Captain Charles C. Wood Taylor and a pair of bronze animals animate an elevation of the living room.

Curtains are deliberately kept
simple with sheer linen hung off
mahogany poles that echo
the waxy finish of the floors.
Underneath, a blue-green roman
shade blends with aquamarine
walls. Dark wood antiques, some
inherited and some picked
up on shopping trips, mix with
new upholstery, providing a
comfortable familiarity between
the past and the present.
A fringed oval ottoman pulls out
for more seating as needed.

PRECEDING SPREAD: The dining room's Gracie mural depicts details from the history of nearby Saint Michaels, Maryland, a maritime town with history that dates to the mid-seventeenth century. Instead of a multicolored or grisaille (gray monotone) palette, Langham requested one in indigo. Cream linen curtains, trimmed in navy blue, frame the window as well as a tufted, kidney-shaped banquette. OPPOSITE: Faded-grass green, vegetable-dyed leather covers a set of chairs from Easton Neston, the English country house in Northamptonshire. The unusually colored Oushak is a favorite of the decorator. "I love it more than anything in the room, except maybe the excellent William IV dining table." ABOVE: When off duty, the sideboard sports a pair of carved mahogany urns and porcelain flower sculptures. Oiled brass sconces strike an early American mood.

OPPOSITE: The hyphen, or breezeway, built to connect the main house to the new garden room, was decorated with the exoticism of the Royal Pavilion at Brighton in mind. Chinese pagoda lanterns light the way, and delicate faux-bamboo settees face off between columns of unlined pale mint linen curtains. ABOVE: A 1920s document pink-and-green-striped wallpaper visually links the breezeway to the colors of the garden room. FOLLOWING SPREAD: Fret for fret, a beloved Sister Parish treillage design was reinterpreted and further animated by *verre-églomisé* birdcages and ceramic parrots. To unify the room, Langham covered all the upholstery in a Kent-Bragaline archival print on custom dark green cretonne, a heavy cotton fabric.

ABOVE: Carved and painted wall lights, topped with tiny pleated shades piped in dark green, flank French doors in the garden room.
OPPOSITE: A pair of Chinese Chippendale chairs pulls up to an English Regency pedestal table while a third sits against the wall until called into service. A painted birdcage on one side of the doorway loosens the symmetry.

In the butler's pantry, historically accurate, old-fashioned American Restoration tiles are laid out with a simple open field, black border, and florets. Glass cabinets are a clever alternative to opaque fronts and essentially allow houseguests to find the wine glasses without having to ask.

ABOVE: A vintage Americana theme threads through the breakfast room with butter-yellow lattice walls, a Formica-topped table, and red fretwork chairs upholstered with blue linen seats. **OPPOSITE:** "The mudroom at Miles-A-Way is the envy of everyone who comes to visit!" laughs Langham. "Never underestimate the allure of a row of hooks and a place for muddy boots." The vanilla beadboard is trimmed in pistachio green. **FOLLOWING SPREAD:** The second-floor stair hall serves as a library antechamber for the bedrooms off it. A magnificent three-quarter-height crotch mahogany, Regency bookcase spans the wall while delicate wheel-backed chairs make themselves available should someone want to peruse a book from the shelves. An octagonal English rent table holds more stacks.

ABOVE: Gray-blue Mauny wallpaper hangs above white painted woodwork up on the third floor in one of Miles-A-Way's nine bedrooms. Since the ceilings are low, the upholstered sleigh bed is intentionally kept close to the floor. Oval-shaped braided wool rugs actually feel contemporary when presented in a new way. OPPOSITE: Langham designed a bench seat with extra storage in the niche created by dormer windows in a third-floor bathroom. Hexagonal, colored penny tiles form an old-fashioned pattern on the floor and correspond to the Wedgewood-blue painted woodwork. FOLLOWING SPREAD: Sparkling water, fields of green grass, and endless blue sky conspire to make Miles-A-Way a paradise at the end of the world.

BRICKS AND BONES

After several years spent in laid-back California, the homeowner, a Tennessee man, began to look eastward again. In fact, he was nostalgic for old-school, Waspy ways—a touch of East Coast rigor.

On a house-hunting trip through Virginia, he found what he was looking for, specifically in the heart of Georgetown, that noble seat of civility. As soon as he saw the handsome Federal house on O Street, standing tall and wide and composed of old, red brick, he just knew this would be the backdrop for the next chapter of his life. With three stories plus an English basement, its rooms were generously proportioned and full of sunlight thanks to original, floor-to-ceiling, six-over-six, double-hung windows.

Langham, who had known the client for years, was summoned to pull it all together. The decorator established a restrained, eighteenth-century Colonial American tenor using stately English and American antiques and archival fabrics. Referencing the Governor's Palace in Williamsburg, an authoritative seriousness was coupled with vivid, saturated hues: tobacco, toffee, burnt sugar, peacock blue, apple green, citron, cantaloupe, mango, and crimson. Antique mantelpieces were acquired and installed—English pine for the living room and a unique, Regency model with a Greek-key motif and tapered columns for the master bedroom. Polished mahogany shutters in the dressing room and fielded paneling applied to one wall of the bedroom—an early American design convention—further enhanced the architectural details.

"We set out to respect the house," Langham says. "Less fluff and more substance." The decorator's well-appointed rooms combined with the client's personal pieces and old family portraits articulated an upright kind of elegance, but were still loose enough to accommodate a few dogs. Precisely the kind of patrician sensibility his client was ready to embrace again.

OPPOSITE: Aristocratic proportions are the hallmark of this three-story, Federal beauty in Georgetown.
FOLLOWING SPREAD: Flawless proportions: the living room is a perfect square with abundant height and light. Twelve-foot-tall windows sport yards of rich sapphire-blue silk fastened to gilded rings on ebonized poles. A nattily dressed Gainsborough chair mingles with other handsomely attired English and American antiques. Ivory silk shades dress a restrained Dutch brass chandelier.

ABOVE: An enormous Joos de Mumper landscape casts a spell over a corner in the living room. An overstuffed chair—one of a pair—is loosely covered in a Clarence House chinoiserie chintz. Toffee-colored satin pillows are hand embroidered. **OPPOSITE:** Scheming commenced with the purchase of a stunning Sultanabad carpet, which reminded the homeowner of one he had seen in the drawing room of England's Howick Hall. With a rare ivory ground, the carpet's faded tones of russet, peacock blue, and mocha thread throughout the house's rice-colored rooms. The English pine mantelpiece was added and crowned with a classic, gilt-wood, convex mirror.

RIGHT: Plaster walls in the dining room are kept creamy while moldings and window surrounds are called out with faux graining, a typical device used in eighteenth-century American interiors. Windows are hung with Chelsea Editions crewel lined in green-on-green gingham. It is, however, the set of comfortable Georgian dining chairs—in burnished-red glove leather with brass nailhead trimming—that commands the room. **FOLLOWING SPREAD:** The master bedroom is thoughtfully composed of cozy upholstery and handsome antiques. The ratcheted English daybed is covered in tobacco chenille and achieves a variety of positions, from upright to flat. The carved-post tester bed has a canopy upholstered with toffee-colored silk gingham, shirred into a sunburst. Heavy curtains made of exotic, mango satin pull across expansive windows, and an angora wool Oushak carpet, woven with autumnal tones, spreads across the floor. The master bedroom's headwall is paneled and glazed in several tones of parchment color. A phantom door, hidden in one of the panels, leads to the dressing room.

ABOVE: Two quilts make up the bed, a gorgeous pumpkin-colored trapunto pulled up over the pillows and an American patchwork folded at the foot. OPPOSITE: Paper-backed, worsted-wool stripes in rich greens create a Saville Row aura in the dressing room. A camel-and-green wool checkerboard carpet covers the floor, and a tufted leather bench is placed at the room's center with closets on three sides.

OPPOSITE: The stair landing between the parlor and the bedroom has just enough room for an exquisite cylinder desk and chair. ABOVE: Emerald cording loops across the window's ebonized pelmet and runs down the edge of the amethyst silk damask curtains, which are finished with tassel fringe.

INFINITE MYSTERY, INFINITE DELIGHT

When shown the Southern colossus to which his client was uprooting from Connecticut, Langham exclaimed, "It's a palace! How will we ever find enough furniture to fit into this place?"

Even though the 1869 Italianate mansion loomed large over New Orleans's Garden District (the front hall itself is ten feet wide), Langham expertly carved out rooms within rooms, furnishing every grand parlor and secret passageway with retro-fitted pieces from his client's previous (Langham-decorated) life and new furniture acquired both locally on Magazine Street and in the French Quarter as well as in Venice, Rome, and Paris. Weaving cultures together, the house has all the exotica—history, mystery, beads, and bourbon—that rightfully belong in this important port city. The opulent plasterwork demanded a degree of formality, as did the homeowner, but the Big Easy also nudged Langham to listen to its *cri de coeur*: "Laissez les bons temps rouler!"

A round dining table positioned in the front parlor facilitates the near-constant hum of parties, seated dinners, and buffet suppers. The voluminous drawing rooms on the right side of the house are thoughtfully outfitted with back-to-back furniture groupings that take the pressure off the scale, driving intimacy. Langham, ever the frustrated couturier, dressed the room's floor-to-ceiling windows in creamy silk, seductively drawn half open day and night. Langham chose a palette of tobacco and duck's-egg blue for the drawing rooms across the hall, creating a kind of sundown refuge. The sheer expanse of fourteen-foot-high plaster walls is a collector's dream; the homeowner (who chairs a contemporary museum in New Orleans) and Langham were able to curate multiple floor-to-ceiling hangings that are always in flux as new pieces come in. Ultimately, Langham bowed down to an elegant kind of decadence—tossing mink throws on armchairs and placing decanters and silver ice buckets at arm's reach—ensuring there is always somewhere cozy to sit and something cold to drink.

Everything about this Samuel Jamison-designed Garden District manse, including the one-hundred-forty-eight-year-old wrought-iron gate that runs the perimeter, conjures the past.

OPPOSITE: In the entrance hall, a coquettish slipper sofa is covered in voided velvet, a type of damask where the visible warp and weft (horizontal and vertical yarns) are juxtaposed against the pile. **ABOVE:** In a mostly tonal hallway, Langham calls attention to the staircase with a burnt-crimson runner, "Whenever I can, I do red up the stairs."

To anchor each side of the white-painted drawing rooms, an enormous Langham-designed rug, which had been used in the owners' California residence, was cut in two. Button tufting and thick tassel fringe embellish back-to-back humpback sofas while rococo armchairs are easy to pull in or out of the conversation.

ABOVE: The background is intentionally monochromatic so that the art powers the narrative. OPPOSITE: Langham conjures a classical interpretation of John Fowler's curtains from Nancy Lancaster's famous London parlor. Fleur-de-lis pleats gather unlined silk fabric, and a double swag of ivory silk cording loosely drapes across the top of the curtains. "Theater-style" Italian stringing permanently catches the curtains on either side for a half-drawn look. Simple striped slipcovers from Tillet Textiles on the four club chairs balance the hauteur of the nineteenth-century plaster cornices.

Golden light filters through the linen scrim curtains and reflects off the gilded carving found all over this most marvelous dining room.

OPPOSITE: Instead of heavy fabric at the dining room's windows, Langham keeps it young, opting for tobacco-colored linen scrim. Eyebrow pelmets, painted obsidian with a gilt edge, accentuate the lines of the arched windows. ABOVE: Everywhere there is a feast for the eyes, especially the intelligent collection of paintings and sculpture acquired over decades of a life spent in the art world.

LEFT: All the key Southern ingredients are here—sparkling crystal, a cabinet of curiosities, rich velvet, and palm fronds—but the secret is the tempered wall color, which mellows the spice. **FOLLOWING SPREAD:** A twelve-foot-long sofa, with enough room for several Penn & Fletcher embroidered pillows, is the heart of the family's primary sitting room. Extra-deep Langham-designed club chairs are slipcovered in striped cotton twill, which Langham puts on damp after washing to avoid shrinkage. The well-worn carpet is a copy designed from a fragment of a Spanish Cuenca.

ABOVE: The master bedroom is deliberately restrained, with a pale French moiré carpet and walls upholstered in muslin that is stamped with a shadowy tree-of-life pattern. OPPOSITE: Like a dash of hot sauce, rich persimmon satin curtains with diamond-smocked valences and bullion fringe sustain the exotic notes.

ABOVE: A Colonial Caribbean scene delights guests in the downstairs powder room. Gilt-wood sconces are a Langham design. OPPOSITE: An unused bedroom is transformed into a luxe dressing-room retreat complete with caned-front closet doors, Hazelton House chintz, and a sumptuous Bessarabian carpet.

FROM BREWTON TO MANHATTAN

"Being brought up in the South taught me something from my very beginnings, something that cannot be learned—
a reverence for home and a pride in our houses, hospitality that is in our DNA."

When he was brought home from the hospital as an infant, Langham's mother remembers thinking, "Isn't it odd? This baby is so alert . . . so wide-eyed . . . looking at *everything.*" She knew on the car ride home that her little boy was really seeing things. Funnily enough, she was right. By the time he was able to move furniture around by himself, he had reassembled his room into a more attractive composition.

Langham's preternatural awareness of architecture and design captivated the local grandes dames of Brewton, Alabama (population five thousand). Early on, Langham's mother and her friends recognized the benefit of having a gifted future-decorator hanging around the house, especially one who would regularly dispense color advice and tell them where their sofas ought to go.

Naturally curious, Langham jumped on every opportunity; his neighbor and early supporter Barbara Blount Lovelace even brought the lanky teen on a road trip to Birmingham to meet renowned Southern decorator Joe McKinnon in hopes of landing him a summer job at the firm. Langham laughs remembering how Barbara was just so commanding, marching him straight into McKinnon's offices, announcing, "Darling, this is Keith Langham. Can't you see he's just the most talented boy in the world!"

He eventually matriculated to the University of Alabama intending to stay put in Tuscaloosa until graduation, but by the beginning of sophomore year he just sensed the glittery beyond beckoning. Langham intuitively knew he'd be better served by soaking up a New York education: "There just weren't a whole lot of options for me in Tuscaloosa. It was time to *go!*"

Fellow Alabamians and fairy god-friends Candy and Bob McMillan generously arranged a trip to New York to transition Keith into his new life up North. Upon arrival in the city, the trio dropped their suitcases at the Carlyle (for an indefinite stay) and Langham hit the pavement— more specifically every floor of the Decorating & Design Building—until he was offered a job in the sample room at Quadrille Fabrics. Simultaneously, he enrolled in night classes at the Fashion Institute of Technology (FIT) and eventually rented a tiny apartment on the Upper East Side. With their young ward's feet firmly planted in Manhattan, the McMillans bid farewell and headed back to Alabama.

If luck and friends appeared to be on Langham's side, so too was excellent timing. In the late 1970s FIT was *the* place to get a good design education. The charismatic chair of the interior-design department, Stanley Barrows, had migrated from Parsons a few years earlier, initiating a grand exodus of teaching talent (under Barrows's aegis, Parsons had minted seminal decorators like Albert Hadley, Angelo Donghia, Mario Buatta, and Thomas Britt).

It was at FIT, specifically in a course called Aesthetics of Design, where Langham says he was taught to really *see.* "In one particular exercise, we were asked to select a room and expound upon what made the composition work.

Richard Keith Langham in the Fifth Avenue dining room of Priscilla Goodrich Rea, who had purchased the apartment from design legend Sister Parish. Langham decorated the rooms while working for Irvine & Fleming.

Even if you hated the room, you were forced to understand *why* it was still successful." By introducing a new way of seeing, the students were pushed to open their eyes to all aesthetics. To this day Langham carries around that concept. "Anyone can say what they *don't* like about a room, but it's much more useful to identify what you *do* like."

BUILDING A STRONG FOUNDATION

With an afternoon off from his duties at Quadrille, Langham took a field trip to the Kip's Bay show house. There, among all the perfectly good and not-so-

ABOVE: Early inspiration: Mark Hampton-designed drawing room at the 1979 Kips Bay Decorator Show House. **OPPOSITE:** The Brewton, Alabama, living room of Candy and Bob McMillan, friends and patrons of the young designer. The McMillan house was Langham's first big project early in his career, completed in 1982.

good installations, was a sitting room dreamed up by Mark Hampton that absolutely knocked him out flat. Ivory cotton slipcovers dressed down serious Regency and William IV antiques while inky-black stippled walls produced a kind of reverse silhouette effect that visually popped the slipcovered shapes against the dark background. The formidable windows were festooned with hopsacking, and sewn-together squares of straw matting covered the floors—at this point no one had ever used sisal in a formal room; in fact no one had ever even *heard* of sisal. The collective result was seriously chic, pivoting traditional design toward the future.

Now that Mark Hampton was on Langham's radar, the next professional move was clear. He launched a letter-writing campaign urging Hampton to consider him for a post. What ensued was a three-month-long exchange of telephone messages and a single interview, but nothing concrete. Then at last, one hot Sunday morning, the phone rang at home. Langham's roommate answered and, gathering that the call was worthy of physical effort, bounded up to the roof where Langham was sunbathing and yelled, "Get down here. Mark Hampton's on the phone!" Langham dashed down the stairs, and picked up the receiver.

"Hello, Keith. It's Mark Hampton."

"Hi!"

"Do you like organ music?"

"Um . . . yes, I do!"

"I'm going to St. John the Divine this afternoon with Lily Auchincloss and Lee Radziwill. We'll pick you up at four o'clock."

The afternoon offered a glimpse into a kind of apprenticeship that would come in due time under the wings of New York's most influential women, but in the more immediate sense Langham got what he desperately desired: a job with a true master. For the next two

years, Keith split his days between the FIT classrooms and the Mark Hampton offices. Even though he was a mere gopher hunting down fabric samples, he was still orbiting Hampton's sun, assimilating firsthand how-tos in courting the most redoubtable clients.

Directly following graduation, Langham went straight to Hampton requesting a full-time job. Rather than offer the twenty-three-year-old a position, Hampton instead suggested time abroad, memorably stating, "Most of what we do is regurgitation—you must go out and build a visual archive upon which to draw."

Hampton generously arranged an introduction with Lady Erica Strong, the legendary design champion responsible for overseeing the handful of applicants selected to attend the prestigious Study Center for the History of Fine and Decorative Arts in London. Langham

was accepted into the program, but had no way to pay the tuition. Once again the McMillans, Langham's old family friends from Alabama, came to the rescue with a ten-thousand-dollar loan. Langham spent the next two years in South Kensington at the "Scout Hut" behind the Victoria and Albert Museum getting a comprehensive design education and haunting practically every grand house across England and France, absorbing the lessons of scale, balance, grandeur, and comfort.

Simultaneously, the budding young designer was building a Rolodex of exceptional European sources including rare antiquarians and the top fabric houses; however, it was during his regular stop-ins at Colefax and Fowler, under the inimitable John Fowler, that he witnessed those elements of aristocratic decorating fused most gloriously.

THE FIRST ASSIGNMENT

Meanwhile back in Alabama, Candy and Bob McMillan had bought Bellemeade, a neoclassical mansion, and were poised to assess the talents of their protégé. They suspected their young friend was more than capable of decorating their new house, but still, they had one critical caveat that must be met: "Get it done fast!" Candy flew to London to meet Keith and together they canvassed every shop on Pimlico Road buying the contents for the house in just two weeks flat. There was no time for second-guessing; upholstery shapes were selected, then dressed in Claremont or Colefax and Fowler fabrics and shipped transatlantic along with furniture and lighting. Back at the house in Brewton, decorative painters and seamstresses toiled around the clock. Chocolate-brown damask curtains tempered painted robin's-egg blue walls in the living room. The dining room was lacquered a deep Chinese red, and the library walls were covered in charcoal Pacific Cloth.

ABOVE: Quintessential Keith Irvine style is evident in a living room he designed on Park Avenue. **OPPOSITE:** The yellow drawing room at 960 Fifth Avenue of Priscilla Goodrich Rea, Langham's "first fancy commission" while working for Irvine & Fleming.

The result was an exuberant expression of creativity driven by momentum and gut instinct.

After the last pillow was tossed and a bouquet of flowers arranged on the entrance-hall table, Langham braced himself for the final reveal, leading the McMillans room by room through their new house. "Bob didn't say a thing," Langham remembers. "After we finished the tour, he brought me straight to the library and, with a huge smile, tore the ten-thousand-dollar promissory note into shreds. I was so relieved they were happy."

Eventually, dwindling funds forced Langham back to America, where he landed in New Orleans on temporary exile from the next chapter of his professional life. He rented a carriage house in the French Quarter and spent a languid summer reconnecting with his Southern roots.

In many ways the rhythms of hospitality in the South echoed the charm and grace of the great rooms of England. In fact, both cultures tended to yield comfortable houses driven by tradition, future criteria by which all Langham interiors would be designed.

Not one to idle in neutral too long, Langham fixated on his next move and ultimately his lazy Southern summer was pierced by trips to New York to interview with the tony firm of Irvine & Fleming. Keith Irvine, originally born in Scotland, had apprenticed with John Fowler in London and was subsequently lured to America to work for Sister Parish, whom he left after less than a year to open his own shop, where he eventually promoted his assistant Tom Fleming to partner. It was here that Langham set his sights.

EARNING HIS STRIPES

The English Country tidal wave finally crashed on American shores in the early '80s and nowhere washed up more ruffles and chintz than Manhattan's Upper

East Side. Armed with a plum position at Irvine & Fleming—the purveyors responsible for that look's most original interiors—Langham once again returned to New York. The partners were terrifically balanced. Langham remembers, "Keith was the flair and Tom was the charisma." Meanwhile, Langham sprang for a small but lavishly decorated apartment jammed with discarded furniture he had picked up from the bountiful streets of the Upper East Side. The *New York Times* thought it all so clever they published it, marking Langham's accidental first foray into promotion.

Langham's tenure at Irvine & Fleming would prominently set the next decade's tone. Here he was disciplined in the concept of nonchalance, a decorating philosophy that produced extravagantly luxe yet lived-in looking rooms seeming to have been passed down from one blue-blooded generation to the next.

Effortless houses don't just happen by themselves. Under Keith Irvine, Langham learned to carefully build

up layers of technique and detail—from a fancy stippled paint job and intricate silk balloon shades hung on gilded rods to a homey needlepoint pillow tossed in an armchair by the fireplace. The sum of a room's fabrics (at least twenty-five or more!) is greater than the whole and though the whole is quite grand, it must always be unpretentious. Selecting a rug that was "slightly off" was the last piece of the puzzle and probably the most germane toward achieving perfect imperfection.

On installation days, assistants would scurry to get every last stick of furniture into place, only to then lug it all to the sides of the room as the antique carpets were brought in. "We'd roll them out one after another, and then place the furniture back into position until Keith eventually chose," Langham remembers. "I always thought, 'Well . . . that one doesn't go!' But of course *that* was the point."

While he was becoming an expert in the field of recherché interiors, Langham was also catering to an astonishingly important roster of clients. Unlike most deans of decorating, Keith Irvine was not at all stingy about introducing Langham to his harem of grand ladies, many of whom were at the apex of New York's social pyramid. Langham was allowed full access to their private, stratified worlds; but more vitally, Langham was being schooled by the best in how to keep a household (or four) humming—a highly disciplined and almost forgotten art.

THE SOPHISTICATING PROCESS

"I want the drawing room to be so bright yellow that you have to wear sunglasses at night!" announced Irvine & Fleming patron Priscilla Goodrich Rea,

ABOVE: Langham with Mrs. William F. Buckley Jr., arriving at the Metropolitan Museum of Art. **OPPOSITE:** The Buckleys' cocoa and crimson drawing room on Park Avenue, designed by Langham circa 1992.

whose maisonette Langham was tasked with decorating (Rea had bought the apartment at 960 Fifth Avenue from Sister Parish, whose bold flourishes, like the checkerboard marble floor, Langham decided to keep). Indeed, Langham chose a Cole & Son printed stripe-on-stripe wallpaper in the most viscous chromium yellow he could find that dialed up all the Directoire and French Empire furniture Rea had cherry-picked from her previous life in Houston.

Rea was an original, but she wasn't the only bright star to cross Langham's path; Irvine & Fleming was a locus of eccentric, intelligent, and chic clientele who were all game-changers in their way. "I was just a sponge, spoiled to be around all these worldly women," Langham says, remembering his good fortune.

Along the way, Langham was cementing his own three-point mantra about decorating: First, timeless rooms always put comfort at the fore. Second, the slavish pursuit of trends would always beget fleeting stagecraft. And third, decoration must distill the essence of the homeowner or, rather, your house should reflect your own style and not your best friend's.

THE GRANDES DAMES

After a year of oddly chance encounters with Jacqueline Kennedy Onassis—many in the elevator of the building that housed both the Irvine & Fleming offices and the fashion showroom of Carolina Herrera, a preferred designer of Onassis—Langham formally met the storied lady. One day, as Langham was at his desk deep into a phone call with a client, the Irvine & Fleming front door buzzed. Rather than the usual fabric-bolt deliveryman, there stood Mrs. Onassis herself wearing giant sunglasses and reflected into glorious infinity in the entry hall's double mirrors. Langham slammed down the receiver. As the elder Keith strolled past the younger Keith's desk,

on his way to the woodworkers in Long Island City. Eight days later, clutching a perfectly turned, electrified, and faux-lacquered column topped with a Colefax and Fowler shade, Langham delivered the matching lamp to Jackie. (In a bookend kind of way, when the pair came up at Sotheby's legendary 1996 auction of all Jackie Onassis's belongings, Langham raised high his paddle and acquired the lamps for eleven thousand dollars.)

From then on, Jackie preferred to work with "the assistant from the elevator." Together, they decorated her cottage in Middleburg, Virginia, poking around thrift shops and "junktiquing." She appreciated the small triumphs, like the twenty-eight-dollar baker's table they stripped down to reveal its natural wood grain. "Don't tell people how much it cost!" she laughed.

Langham worked with Jackie Kennedy Onassis on her Manhattan apartment for several years, primarily sprucing up rooms with textiles, paints, and wall coverings that were similar to ones used in earlier schemes: curtains with hand-painted blue stripes on ivory silk gazar **(upper left)**, originally designed by John Fowler and replaced by Langham circa 1990, and "Les Tuileries" fabric from Scalamandré **(above)** for bed hangings. **OPPOSITE:** One of many notes from Onassis to the designer, circa 1988.

he smiled and said, "Come on now, I know you're dying to meet her . . . "

"Jackie, this is Richard Keith Langham, my talented young assistant."

Sunglasses tilted up and a sly smile of recognition. "Oh, yes . . . my friend from the elevator." Sunglasses back down. "I'm giving a party, and I need a new lamp. The pair I got in Greece have never been quite right. Do you have another one like *this*?"

Whether or not a matching lamp existed, Langham replied, "Yes! Yes, we do!"

"Wonderful! Please have it brought by as soon as you can."

As soon as Jackie left, a bewildered Keith Irvine said, "What the hell, Richard?" (At work, Keith Langham was referred to by his first name, Richard, to avoid confusion with the elder Keith Irvine.)

Like a shot, Langham was out the door, in a taxi

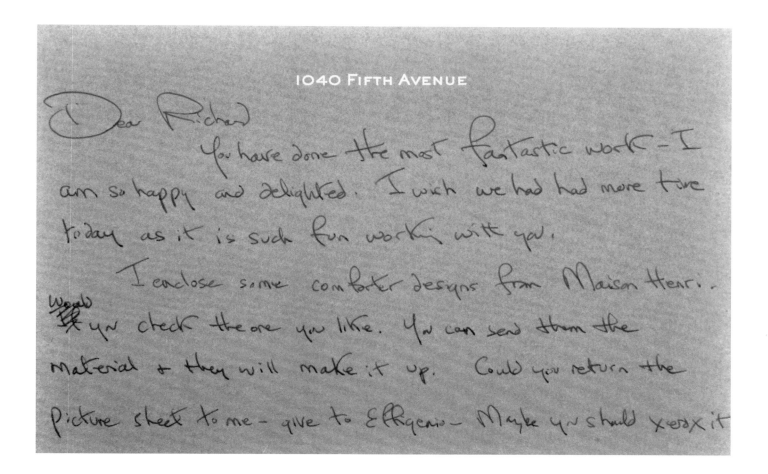

Dear Richard,
    You have done the most fantastic work – I am so happy and delighted. I wish we had had more time today as it is such fun working with you.
    I enclose some comforter designs from Maison Henri. Would you check the one you like. You can send them the material + they will make it up. Could you return the picture sheet to me – give to Effigenia – Maybe you should xerox it

Langham also helped Jackie to fluff 1040 Fifth Avenue over the years; she even called him in at the eleventh hour to replace the tattered silk bed hangings that she had deemed too expensive to redo, but finally sprang for, literally in the last months of her life.

At this point, it was obvious Langham was more than capable of holding his own, so much so that Keith and Tom weren't sure how much longer he'd stick around. In an effort to engage their now-head designer, they generously tossed the crème de la crème of society his way. But by his ninth year there, the curtain was closing. Subsequently, Mr. and Mrs. William F. Buckley Jr. were to be his last clients at Irvine & Fleming and the first at Richard Keith Langham Interiors. "To this day, Tom and I regret losing Pat Buckley," Keith Irvine later said when asked about Langham's inevitable departure. "But we knew Richard was more her *tasse de thé*."

Langham cites Pat Buckley as the sort of end-all dream client, his ultimate Auntie Mame. The Buckleys themselves set a standard against which all social behavior in Manhattan was measured, owing in part to Pat's unshakeable sense of self. "She and Bill were profoundly erudite. She had a glamour that was intangible and above fashion," remembers Langham. "You would have one meeting with Pat and in five minutes she would make all the decisions to move a project forward…'Let's go with yellow chintz, tangerine lacquer walls, and match the lampshades to my panty hose!' Today you'd have to hem and haw for six months in order to come to the same conclusion with a client." Part of that self-assuredness was a response to the times. Pat Buckley wasn't curled up in her red library cruising through thousands of wallpaper samples online; rather she trusted her decorator to do that for her so she could contribute to her other passions.

LANGHAM
& COMPANY

ROARING FIRES AND AFTERNOON TEA

In 2000, the decorator finally hung his shingle out in front of what he refers to as "The Bank." Originally built as a pawnshop in the 1930s, the cavernous space morphed into the Provident Loan Society and eventually turned into an abandoned historic hunk of brownstone in total disrepair. But still, Langham could not resist the thirty-foot vaulted ceilings, Palladian windows, and multiple fireplaces (nonfunctioning from neglect). A massive restoration ensued and the main room was transformed into a Nancy Lancaster-esque butter-yellow dream out of which Langham sold his eponymous line of upholstered furniture and antiques. Located on East 60th Street across from Bloomingdale's, the Bank—with its fireplaces roaring again and tea served every day at four o'clock—was almost too attractive. Before long Langham's friends and clients started to arrive in droves around three-thirty and permanently install themselves in deep armchairs, chattering away until it was dark out. A secret rope ladder was installed in the back so that Langham, ever the polite host, could climb out the window undetected, scale down the side of the building, and escape via the basement of the building, next door to go knock out his deadlines before end of day.

AN OLD-FASHIONED FUTURE

Having been in the business over thirty years, Langham has never wavered from his original commitment to respecting tradition and honoring the best of what's come before us. That continuity of history is present throughout the body of his work, purposefully lending a familiarity that speaks directly to our creature comforts.

Langham believes traditional rooms do not appear instantaneously—they mature. He is a measured maximalist whose intention is for your eye to be stimulated, to land here and there on beauty or substance or even a little something to put you in a jolly frame of mind the minute you cross the threshold from the demanding "out there" to the comfort of "in here." Langham's desire is to cosset you in relaxed grandeur.

What you will always find in Langham's world are good English and American antiques, exquisitely upholstered armchairs and sofas, yards of couturier curtains that look as good from outside as they do inside, and well-placed mementos all arranged against a colorful background. Children and dogs are welcome, and televisions hide in plain sight. A fire is likely roaring in the fireplace and a gilded mirror might hang over the mantel where you can easily glance at your hair.

Whether any of these elements is the lead actor or just has a few lines, each piece plays a role in Langham's theater of the chic. As the director says, "All the bits work together to give the story dimension, character, and a past, but it's the people in the room that provide the drama!"

ABOVE: The designer's business card depicted the façade of the Langham & Company showroom on East 60th Street in New York City. **OPPOSITE:** Keith reminisces about the showroom's interior, "I was the only person in town with my own ballroom."

IF THESE WALLS COULD TALK

Keith has created five beautiful houses for me and my family over the past two decades. The experience has always been joyful, often hilarious, and definitely filled with hijinks.

Funnily enough, each of the houses featured in this book belongs to a dear friend of Keith's (they are never simply just clients), many whom are friends of mine now. Keith's brilliant humor is infectious, and we all find he makes us cleverer and funnier than we ever would have been without his friendship. My children even admit we would be far more boring without this artistic delight in our lives. Working with Keith is an education—he aspires to a higher aesthetic without allowing that aesthetic to become his raison d'être. Embedded in his genius is an essential authenticity that makes all of his interiors welcoming and comfortable while still being utterly glamorous. In addition to creating refined homes, Keith also brings his uncompromising style to commercial projects. Brennan's entrusted Keith with restoring their beloved restaurant back to its chic heyday, and Verdura had the designer create their elegant showroom in New York. But truly, people and friendships matter most to Keith. He has always been eager to promote and help one and all, mentoring an entire generation of young designers and artisans.

If these walls could talk—besides telling naughty stories—the curtains, the fabrics, the custom carpets, and the myriad of details, along with the graciousness he has given us all, would say, "Thank you!"

—Allison Kendrick
New Orleans, Louisiana

ACKNOWLEDGMENTS

I thank the following people for helping with this book and my career:

Candy and Bob McMillan for giving me the BIGGEST gift of all—New York City.

Mark Hampton, through whom I first saw masterful decoration.

Keith Irvine and Tom Fleming, who were generous and brave to teach me, believe in me, and make life-changing introductions.

Charles Miers, who from across a dinner table invited me to do this book with Rizzoli.

Philip Reeser, whose diligence and vision made all of this material come together.

Sara Ruffin Costello, my Southern compatriot, who understood me and, with her own magic, turned my endless babbling into elegant prose.

Doug Turshen and David Huang, who designed a beautiful book.

Trel Brock, Pieter Estersohn, Erik Kvalsvik, Francesco Lagnese, Eric Piasecki, William Waldron, and the late Fernando Bengoechea, whose photographic talents made all these pages look rich.

Barbara Burton, Cece Cord, Lisa Fine, Allison Kendrick, Kinsey Marable, John Mayfield, Angele Parlange, Mary Pezzaro, and Alease Fisher Tallman, who listened ad nauseam to my ideas and opinions—while I squelched theirs!

Lewis Graeber III, who so often brought me on board to furnish his exquisite houses.

MLD, my BFF among other things.

Mary Bond Bailey, who has contributed her tech and graphics savvy.

Terry Stevenson, who has been my bedrock and who moves my mountains.

My eager and willing assistants, who helped make these rooms happen: Margaret Moore Chambers, Lindsey Coral Harper, Maggie Scott Currey, Elizabeth Cleary, Kathryn Tatum Saunders, John Craver, Mary Caroline Clifton Mumpower, Lorri Hicks, Julia Mason, Lindsey Kelley, Louise Marsh, Vernona Tambke Pappas, Betsy Blackman, and Anne Taylor Whitney Cooper.

The artisans and craftsmen who contributed their skills without which these rooms would be empty.

Michael Boodro, Howard Christian, Carolyn Englefield, Margaret Russell, Clinton Smith, and Lydia Somerville—the keen-eyed editors who published my work in their magazines.

Carolyn, Warren, Follin, John, Allison, Bill, Bruce, Emmy, Sue, John, Mollie, Billy, Alease, Suzanne, Ramsey, Blaine, and Steve, who opened their doors (and their bank accounts) and allowed me to create.

PHOTOGRAPHY CREDITS

All images copyright © by Trel Brock except for the following:

The Studio at Fernando Bengoechea: 155, 156, 157, and 158–59

Fernando Bengoechea / Getty Images: 88, 92–93, 95, 96–97, 98–99, 153, 154, 160, and 161

David Connell: 248 (left)

Pieter Estersohn: 9, 10, 11, 15, 16, 16–17, 19, 24, 25, 28–29, 87, 89, 94, 100, 101, 102, and 103

David Frazier: 247

Lizzie Himmel: 241

Erik Kvalsvik: 59, 60–61, 62, 63, 64–65, 66–67, 68, 69, 206, 208–9, 210–11, 212–13, 214–15, 216, 217, 218, and 219

Francesco Lagnese: 71, 72–73, 74–75, 76, 77, 78, 79, 80, 81, 82–83, and 84–85

Courtesy of Langham & Company: 243, 246, 249, and 250

Eric McNatt: 251

Michael Mundy: 244 and 245

Eric Piasecki / OTTO: 4, 133, 134–35, 136, 137, 138–39, 140–41, 142–43, 144, 145, 146, 147, 148–49, 150, and 151

Peter Vitale: 242

William Waldron: 105, 106–7, 108, 108–9, 110, 111, 112–13, 114–15, 163, 164–65, 166, 172–73, 222, 224–25, 228–29, and 233–34

First published in the United States of America in 2017 by

Rizzoli International Publications, Inc.
300 Park Avenue South
New York, NY 10010
www.rizzoliusa.com

Philip Reeser, Editor
Barbara Sadick, Production Manager
Elizabeth Smith, Copy Editor

Design by Doug Turshen with David Huang
Printed and bound in China
2017 2018 2019 2020 / 10 9 8 7 6 5 4 3 2 1